THE
S
DRUNKS

A YEAR'S WORTH OF REAL-LIFE DRUNKEN MAYHEM FROM THE WORLD'S NEWS

CHRIS PILBEAM

Crombie Jardine
PUBLISHING LIMITED

13 Nonsuch Walk, Cheam, Surrey, SM2 7LG
www.crombiejardine.com

This edition was first published by Crombie Jardine
Publishing Limited in 2005

ISBN 1-905102-23-2

Written by Chris Pilbeam
Designed by www.mrstiffy.co.uk
Printed and bound in the United Kingdom by
William Clowes, Beccles, Suffolk

ABOUT THE AUTHOR

Chris Pilbeam is the News
Editor at *Front Magazine*

and is responsible for writing and commissioning pieces ranging from celebrity interviews to humorous and news-related stories.

One of Chris' hobbies is gathering snippets of international news, regularly searching up to a hundred websites for the cream of the world's local reports.

This, combined with living in

London's majestic Holloway Road area, where Chris says he spends "a lot of time stepping out of the way of drunk people", has lead to *The Little Book of Stupid Drunks: A Year's Worth of Real-Life Drunken Mayhem from Around the World*.

INTRODUCTION

We've all woken up after a few drinks with the nagging feeling that we did something silly last night. We all know the feeling of hung-over panic as we try to mentally piece together the jigsaw pieces of the previous evening. If we're lucky, we're worrying about nothing. If we're unlucky, we'll have to deal with the consequences of

blabbing a trusted secret,
avoid a colleague for a month
or explain to a neighbour
why their garden now
contains a supermarket
trolley full of gnomes.

Some of us are unluckier than
others. Some people have
to learn that they stole an
aeroplane and took it for a
joyride, or that they drove a
car into a police station, or that
they tried to outrun a police car

on a tractor, or that they broke
into their local radio station
and held the DJ hostage with an
airgun. It's these people who
are the stars of this book.

I've been collecting their
stories for a year now. These
people aren't film stars
renowned for their party
lifestyles, by the way. They're
just you and me after five or
six or seven drinks too many.
They didn't know what was

going to happen. It probably seemed like a great idea at the time. I love these stories because they could technically have happened to any one of us. Apart from the one about the drunk Thai man who claimed that the stray dog was 'acting sexy'. That's just wrong.

Cheers.

BOOZE BREAKS DOWN BARRIERS BETWEEN GUARD AND INMATE

A deputy jailer from Kentucky, USA, found himself in the same cell as the inmate he was supposed to be driving to prison after the pair got

drunk en route and decided
to make a spot of cash by
'fining' other motorists.

Deputy Jailer Clarence Wilson
left the Knox County jail
with inmate Shawn Reynolds
handcuffed in the back seat, a
court later heard. Somewhere
along the way, Reynolds
ended up in the front seat,
swigging alcohol with Wilson.
In nearby Fayette County, the
pair began stopping speeding

motorists and 'arresting' them; detaining them in the back of the officially-marked car, making on-the-spot cash fines, and letting them go.

Spoilsport cops put the brakes on their money-making idea after several motorists reported two drunk men making traffic stops. Wilson was jailed for three years after being charged with drink driving, impersonating a police officer, unlawful imprisonment and official misconduct.

DRINKING COMPETITION LEAVES BAD TASTE IN MAN'S MOUTH

Many of us have woken up after a heavy night with a nasty taste in our mouths. Twenty-two-year old Tony McGee, of Brisbane, Australia, probably thought nothing was out of the

ordinary until someone told him
that he had bitten off the tail
a live mouse in order to win a
competition in his local pub.

McGee had no recollection of
doing this, a court was later
told – he only remembered
'having a mouse in his
possession'. Charged with
cruelty to an animal, McGee
recalled having drunk a pint
of anchovies, eaten a cup
of maggots and set off a

mouse trap with his tongue after downing whisky and beer for six hours prior to the competition. He emerged the eventual winner after the runner-up spat out his mouse.

Expressing his remorse, McGee pleaded guilty and was fined the equivalent of £200. We don't know what his prize for winning the competition was.

WINE THEFT PROVES A SICKENING SPECTACLE

Caught red-handed with a stolen bottle of wine and cornered, a 19-year old German drunk took the only honourable course of action – he gulped the lot before anyone could take it from him. Within seconds, he began spraying vomit like a busted hosepipe over everyone present.

He'd actually downed a wine bottle full of vinegar that the landlady of the bar in Scwabach, Germany, had left on the counter as a trap after seeing the light-fingered lush pilfer a couple of bottles earlier.

"I guess he thought he'd better make the most of it," explained the arresting officer, who arrived to find the thief pinned to the ground, still retching, having lost his entire

day's haul of stolen wine onto
the shoes of his captors.

DRUNK FAILS TO SCORE WITH DOG

A 33-year old Thai man who got
drunk and tried to rape a dog
had to flee his home to avoid
the ridicule of his neighbours.
On the way home from an
all-day drinking session at a
friend's house, 33-year old

Toryip Rawang spotted the stray female dog wagging her tail and 'acting sexy'.

"I always become aroused when I drink heavily," Toryip Rawang explained to police who picked him up. "But I did not have enough money to pay a prostitute."

He bundled the animal into long grass by the roadside but it resisted, biting him in

the face, chest and arms. Locals called police when they saw him staggering down the road covered in his own blood. Toryip received several painful rabies injections, and later admitted to raping three other dogs while drunk.

GOVERNMENT OFFICIAL MISUSES EMERGENCY EXIT IN FRONT OF HIS BOSS

A government press officer in the Philippines had to apologise to President Gloria Macapagal Arroyo after drunkenly urinating in the emergency exit of the presidential aircraft. Heraclio Nazareno consumed so much booze on a state flight back from Paris that he mistook the emergency exit for the toilet.

Nazareno later wrote to the president expressing 'regret' over the incident. At the time of the report, she had not yet decided whether to punish him, but insiders at the presidential palace said that he was likely to be posted to a new job somewhere far, far away.

ROBBER BECOMES VICTIM OF HIS OWN SUCCESS

An armed robber from the Finnish town of Turku was cursing his thirst for booze after a bottle of spirits landed him in hot water.

The 32-year old robber stormed into a hotel in the small hours of the morning, where he threatened the

receptionist with a weapon
and emptied the till. He then
demanded several bottles
of spirits, and ordered the
receptionist out to a cash point
to withdraw money for him.

On the way to the cash point,
however, the robber sank so
much of his stolen liquor that
he passed out on the spot,
leaving it to the taxi driver and
the receptionist to drop him
off at the local police station.

RUSSIAN MP GOES NUCLEAR ON COPS

When a patrol car in Moscow was flagged down by three drunk men late at night, the officers inside were surprised to recognise two of them as Vladislav Demin; a member of the Russian parliament, and Alexi Kozertsky, his secretary. They were doubly surprised when Demin charged into them after they got out of

their car. Screaming 'beat
the cops', the MP laid out
one officer with a punch to
the face before Kozertsky
steamed in, swinging two
baseball bats that he'd stolen
out of a car parked nearby.

When the battling politicians
were finally overpowered, Demin
pulled out his MP's identity
card, claimed immunity from
prosecution and walked off,
leaving the loyal Kozertsky to

face the music. The Russian Liberal and Democratic Party refused to comment on the actions of their MP, explaining that the leader of the party was on holiday.

POLICE OFFICERS FAIL TO SET THE BEST EXAMPLE TO OTHER DRIVERS

An American police chief has sent a warning to all officers

in the Minneapolis area about inappropriate behaviour at Christmas parties after five of his officers were arrested in eight months - for driving while intoxicated. Four of them were arrested for simple drink driving. The fifth was arrested for driving the wrong way down a busy Minneapolis city street after a party and then pulling his gun on a member of the public.

HUNGRY DRUNK DEFIES TRAINS FOR CAKE

"I wanted to buy some cakes, but the store on platform 1 was closed," Tadakazu Mitshui explained to police who found him stumbling across high-speed train tracks in Hiroshima, Japan. "So I crossed the tracks to buy them on the other platform." Tadakazu, who admitted to having had a pint or three, wanted cake at all costs.

Station staff and commuters watched in horror as the 41-year old restaurant owner staggered across 220mph 'bullet train' tracks at Hiroshima station. They decided to call police when Tadakazu, proudly clutching his cakes, began clambering onto the tracks again for the return leg of his mission. Cops turned up in time to haul him back onto the platform and arrest him.

The fate of his cakes remains unknown.

DRUNK IN CHARGE OF A STREET SWEEPER

It was a quiet night for police officers in the little American town of Macomb, Illinois, until 21-year old Brian Tardi got tired of walking home after a night's drinking. Officers were surprised to see Tardi, shirtless and clutching a broken mobile phone, rumbling through the town on a street sweeper. Luckily the sweeper ran out of petrol a few hundred yards down the road, averting the possibility of a 15mph police chase.

DRUNK BURGLAR RAIDS FRIDGE

When a resident of the town of Bluffton in South Carolina heard a noise from downstairs in the middle of the night, he feared the worst. Creeping downstairs to confront the intruder, he burst into his kitchen to find a 36-year old man sitting on the floor, drunk, gobbling cold fried chicken from the refrigerator.

Apprehended at gunpoint by police who arrived on the scene, the peckish prowler admitted he was drunk but claimed that he knew the resident of the home. Cunningly, an officer asked the burglar what the homeowner's name was. "Oh well, you got me," shrugged the peckish prowler. He was hauled off to jail to be charged with trespassing and the theft of $10 worth of chicken.

DRUNK LAWYER PLEADS GUILTY

"I think I should be reported," a top British lawyer shrugged after admitting to being 'drunk as a monkey' during a court case in Hong Kong. Roderick Murray apparently had a few beers at lunchtime and when he returned to court, he was seen to be laughing, clapping, drumming his fingers on the table, and wearing a pair of sunglasses. The judge eventually had to adjourn the case after Murray began mumbling while the defence summed up its case.

"You have to hear a lot of bullshit in court," explained the legal eagle after the hearing, which resumed after officials had given him a stern talking-to.

DRUNK DRIVER DECIDES NOT TO PAY FOR PETROL

When police in Des Moines, Iowa, saw a car speed away from a garage forecourt, they assumed that the driver had done a runner without paying and set off in pursuit.

However, 19-year old Cory Kellow didn't want to stop. He sped into the town of Indianola, where he crashed into a ditch

before speeding out again and
onto the highway at 100mph,
triggering a huge police chase.
After several miles and the
wreckage of one patrol car,
Kellow finally rolled into a ditch,
where officers dragged him
from the driver's seat with
'bloodshot, watery eyes, slurred
speech and a strong odour of
alcohol.' Having been handcuffed,
Kellow decided to fight his way
out of custody, which in reality
involved him weakly kicking

the officers several times.

Having finally been bundled into a patrol car, Kellow played his trump card – telling officers that the state's drink driving laws didn't apply to him because he didn't have a driving licence.

40

JUDGE UNIMPRESSED BY DRUNK DEFENDANT

When you're due in court on your third drink-driving charge, it's probably best not to drink before you get there. This doesn't appear to have occurred to 52-year old Larry Ardoin of Louisiana, USA, who showed up to his trial smelling of alcohol and slurring his words. Asked by the judge if he'd been drinking,

Ardoin answered, "Judge, I'm from Mamou!" - referring to a Louisiana town infamous for its riotous Mardi Gras celebrations.

Unimpressed, the prosecutor ordered a blood test that showed Ardoin was three times over the drink-driving limit. He returned to the court sober that afternoon to plead guilty to his original charge.

DRUNK BRITON FINDS INGENIOUS PLACE TO HIDE ILLEGAL FIREARM

A British drinker will be spending the next few years behind bars after shooting himself in the testicles with a sawn-off shotgun.

Twenty-eight-year old David Walker was arguing with a friend in the local boozer about whose turn it was to buy the

16th pint when he decided to resolve the argument by going home and fetching the illegal weapon. On his way back to the pub, which by then was closed, Walker stuffed the firearm into his pants, where it went off accidentally.

Despite managing to hide the gun in a litter bin and crawl home, Walker, of Sheffield, was arrested and sentenced to five years for possession of a prohibited firearm. He told police that he was so drunk he couldn't remember why he did any of it.

Unsuccessfully pleading for mercy, Walker's solicitor Gulzar Sayed pointed out to the court that his client still feels severe pain, and that several pellets remain lodged in his scrotum.

FATHER CHRISTMAS GETS ARRESTED

Father Christmas is supposed to enter houses through the chimney, not the front door - so residents of one quiet American neighbourhood can be forgiven for calling the police when they saw a 50-year old drunk in a Santa suit trying to barge into someone's house. The suspect wandered off before the police arrived, but was apprehended

at the wonderfully-named
Kronenberg Trailer Park
where, in a terrible blow for
the spirit of Christmas, this
particular Santa was arrested
for his seventh offence of
public intoxication and for
possession of marijuana.

DRUNK GARDENING PROVES COSTLY

An American man has been
fined the equivalent of £500
for driving a lawnmower
while drunk. Forty-five-year
old Barry Davis was spotted
weaving along a street in the
town of Hartford, Wisconsin,
and was arrested after failing
'sobriety tests' – the delightful
rituals in which suspected
drunks are made to stand on

48

one leg and recite the alphabet
backwards. Davis admitted
to drinking seven beers, but
claimed that he didn't think
that being drunk in charge of
a lawnmower was illegal.

BEAR DEVELOPS DRINK PROBLEM

Bears in the USA's National
Parks are known for their
tendency to be light-fingered

around tourist's food supplies.
It was realised that a bear in
the state of Washington had
gone one step further when
it was found passed out on
the front lawn of a campsite
in the resort of Baker Lake.
Scattered across the lawn were
no less than 36 empty cans
of beer that it had pilfered,
clawed open, and drunk.

When a park ranger attempted
to chase it away, the bear

could barely move except to drag itself up a tree where it fell asleep for four hours. Rangers managed to capture it the next day by baiting a trap with doughnuts... and two more cans of beer.

RUSSIAN CABIN CREW TURN THE TABLES (UPSIDE DOWN)

Perhaps fed up of drunken

passengers causing all
the trouble on aeroplanes,
two crew members on a
Russian airliner decided to
get involved themselves.

Passengers first noticed
something was amiss when the
stewards only began catering
to them an hour and a half into
the domestic Aeroflot flight.
When the food finally came out,
reported one passenger, the
stewards were so drunk that

half of it ended up on the floor.
Concerned by this, a passenger
named as Mr. Chernopup
demanded to be served by 'a
sober and competent flight
attendant.' Stung by the
accusation, two crew members
leapt on Chernopup and roughed
him up in full view of everyone.

The entire flight crew has
been temporarily dismissed
pending an investigation.

BOOZE DEFENCE FAILS TO GET ROBBER OFF THE HOOK

A convicted bank robber in New Mexico, USA, tried a novel way to get his conviction overturned: arguing that he was too drunk at the time to be held responsible.

The proof? Fifty-seven-year old Raymond Hernandez claimed that his crime was clearly so stupid that only a severely drunk person would have tried it. He had gone into a bank after a drinking session and tried to cash a cheque. When the cashier refused, Hernandez came back a few minutes later and attempted to rob the very same cashier.

Under New Mexico state law, drunkenness can sometimes be used as a defence. However, the state Court of Appeals refused to overturn the conviction, noting that not everyone who gets drunk does this sort of thing.

DRUNKEN PRANK-CALLER DEMONSTRATES IMPRESSIVE COMMITMENT

A Japanese man has been arrested for making 9,000 prank telephone calls to police while drunk. Unemployed Takashi Kikuchi, 59, of Tokyo, made 64 hours worth of emergency calls over a three-month period. He would either swear at the operators or rant about the deployment of Japanese soldiers in Iraq. He is being prosecuted for obstructing police from carrying out their duty.

MAN CELEBRATES COMING OF AGE IN STYLE

In the USA the legal drinking age is 21, and the 21st birthday is a cause for some celebration. Louis Paul Kadlecek of Texas celebrated his with a four-day drinking binge, before deciding to try something a little different - flying to Mexico in a stolen aeroplane.

Kadlecek wandered onto his

local airfield, climbed into a
plane and took it for a spin
around the runway. Deciding,
however, that the plane was
beyond his capacity to fly,
Kadlecek broke into a smaller
plane, loaded a crate of beer
into the seat next to him and
headed down the runway again.
He managed to take off and
fly for about a mile before
slicing through some power
lines and crashing in a field.
Amazingly, he was unhurt, and

managed to walk the three miles back to his house.

Kadlecek would have got away with it if several people hadn't witnessed the crash and described him to police. When the cops arrived at his house, the birthday boy had already packed his toothbrush for a long stay in jail.

DRUNK DRIVER FAILS TO GET A JOB WITH HIGHWAY PATROL

A 25-year old American failed to get into his local police force in spectacular fashion after drinking an extremely potent Long Island Iced Tea cocktail before driving to his local station to enquire about a job.

According to police officers, Robert Gulley wandered into

the Washington State Patrol
headquarters glassy-eyed,
slurring his words and smelling
of alcohol. When asked how he'd
got to the police station, Gulley
claimed to have been given a
lift. Suspicious, officers sent
him home with a warning not to
drive. Gulley was then observed
thoughtfully pacing backwards
and forwards outside the
station for ten minutes before
sneakily jumping into his car and
driving off. He was instantly

pulled over and ticketed.

The incident has reportedly only strengthened Gulley's desire to join the police department. He may, however, have difficulty in doing so. "I guarantee he's not going to get a job with us," said a State Patrol spokesman.

DENTIST'S APPOINTMENT GOES FROM BAD TO WORSE

A Leeds dentist found himself suspended after a lunchtime drinking session caused him to collapse on a patient.

The General Dental Council heard that 45-year old Colin McKay had drunk six glasses of wine before attempting work on the mouth of one Andrea

Harrison. He collapsed on her, breaking one of her teeth and forcing her to wriggle out from underneath him. "He was sweating and I tried to get him off me," recalled Mrs Harrison. "He was pinning me down and I could smell the alcohol."

McKay was found guilty of serious professional misconduct. "It was the most terrifying thing I have ever been through in my life," Mrs Harrison later told the press. "I didn't like going before, but I certainly don't want to go again."

MUM DROPS HERSELF IN IT

A 35-year old Australian woman was arrested for drink driving in record time after ploughing her car through the fence of her local police station. Police

in the town of Eskdale were on
the scene in seconds to deal
with the wrecked mum-of-
three, who was unhurt until she
became unruly and had to be
subdued with pepper spray.

DRUNK IN CHARGE OF A DONKEY CART

A South African man was
fined the equivalent of £200
after being caught, twice in

the same day, being drunk in charge of a donkey cart.

Hans du Toit was stopped in the town of Philipolis when police officers noticed that his cart was swerving all over the town's one main road and told him not to continue. Sneaky Hans, however, kept on going as soon as the police left. "When the policeman left," he later testified in court, "I decided: 'I know this road and so do my

68

donkeys. If I don't find the way home, my donkeys will.'"

Unfortunately, after continuing to swerve in and out of the road, he was stopped for a second time. His wife was called to take the animals home while Hans took a trip to the police station.

POLAR BEAR TAKES THE BISCUIT AND MORE

A 31-year old Estonian pulled off an impressive drunken double after a session with friends in the capital Tallinn. Clambering into the zoo in search of a place to sleep would have sufficed, but he went the extra mile upon waking up when he tried to feed a polar bear a biscuit he found in his pocket. The bear wasn't content with just the biscuit, though, and bit off the man's entire hand.

Worryingly, the zoo's manager said that it was the 11th time that this had happened in his 30 years of working there.

DRUNK PRIEST SETTLES ARGUMENT IN UNGODLY FASHION

A priest in Zagreb, Croatia, is

in trouble with the law after a meal at a restaurant with members of his parish turned ugly. After a few glasses of wine an argument occurred, which Father Josef Stefancic resolved by smacking one of his flock in the face, pulling out a rifle, threatening everyone else in the room with it, and fleeing in his car.

Stefancic didn't get far before wrapping his car around a

tree. When police arrived, he
refused to take a breath test.
His bishop has defended him,
explaining to the press that
Stefancic didn't act alone – the
wine was equally responsible.

"I must admit that I made
a mistake," said Stefancic
after the incident. "However,
everyone makes mistakes, even
politicians and the pope."

DRUNK DISPLAYS
ADMIRABLE HONESTY

A 28-year old drunk driver from the rural state of Vermont in the USA was arrested after pulling up alongside a police car and telling the officer, "I've been looking for someone to arrest me. I'm drunk."

SLEEPY DRUNK DECIDES THAT ANY BED WILL DO

When 50-year old Harold Ballantine of Ipswich found himself out and drunk at night, he just wanted to curl up in bed. And he wasn't bothered about whose bed it was.

Ballantine knocked on the door of a complete stranger at 3am on a Thursday morning. When the owner of the house came downstairs, he barged past her and went to bed in her room. The mortified woman called the police, who found Ballantine asleep. When they pulled the duvet off him, he thrashed around, kicked one officer and revealed to all present that he had removed his underpants prior to bedding down.

"This is amusing on one hand," Ballantine's defence lawyer told Suffolk Magistrates Court,

"but I appreciate the lady
must have been horrified. The
defendant went to the bed
simply with a view of sleeping
there and I think he is now
ashamed of what he did."

The judge ordered Ballantine
to be jailed for 28 days
but declined to make him
pay compensation. "I don't
imagine either the police or
the victim want your money,"
he explained. "They just want

to never see you again."

TEENAGE SWEDES INVENT A VERY CLEAN NEW COCKTAIL

When Anders Persson, provider of portable toilets to a Swedish music festival, noticed that the liquid soap from his toilets was vanishing at a rate of knots, he smelt a rat. "It took only one night for most of it to disappear," he remembered later. "It usually lasts for a month."

When a teenage girl was admitted to a local hospital with alcohol poisoning, things became clearer. She explained to doctors that the younger festival-goers had realised that Persson's soap has a 62 percent alcohol content, and that they'd been mixing it with Red Bull to get smashed on the cheap.

DRUNK RUSSIAN TAKES NAUTICAL JOYRIDE

Police in Venice feared a terrorist attack was taking place when one of the city's famous water buses began hurtling through canals at high speeds, capsizing gondolas and executing high-speed turns. Rather than a terrorist

at the controls, however,
the culprit was a drunk
Russian sailor on a joyride.

When the boat headed in the
direction of a petrochemical
plant, panicking police were
scrambled to prevent a
suicide bombing. As they drew
alongside the waterbus the
driver turned and tried to
ram them, but the officers
managed to avoid a collision and
eventually managed to stop

the waterbus by leaping onto
it and overpowering the driver,
who was arrested for breaking
navigation rules, the theft of
a boat and resisting arrest.

DRUNK TEACHER WRECKS HIS OWN SCHOOL, THEN GETS WRECKED HIMSELF

Cambodian teacher Long
Rumchek had an unusual habit.

When he got drunk, he would usually go back to the school where he worked to smash its windows. "He always disturbs and destroys school property when he gets drunk," explained exasperated Kampong Bay police chief Nhem Huon. On the last occasion, however, he didn't get away with it – he was severely beaten up by a 17-year old girl.

Hor Chenda, one of Rumchek's

students, who lives next door to the school and whose father is the school's security guard, had had enough. Rather than waking up her dad, she went round there with a metre-long stick and battered the wretched Rumbek until he was thoroughly concussed.

The local community has taken her side, agreeing that Rumchek, who has been repeatedly reprimanded for wrecking the school while drunk, probably had it coming.

DRUNK NUN CAUSES UNHOLY SCENE

A Polish nun is in a spot of trouble after police claimed she drunkenly ploughed a tractor into a car in the town of Dzierzoniow. Despite being in 'no fit state to blow into a breathalyser', according to arresting officers, the 45-year old nun was eventually tested and allegedly found to be a spectacular 17 times over Poland's drink-driving limit.

DRUNK PILOT INSPIRES NEW LAW

A pilot who took a dangerous drunken spin over the city of Philadelphia not only received six months in jail but had the honour of a new law being written to deal with anyone who follows his example in the future. John Salamone's four-hour joyride while twice over the drink-driving limit has inspired Pennsylvania's new Flying While Impaired Bill, which will make flying while drunk punishable by jail.

"It was just a mess," said prosecutor John Gradel at Salamone's trial. "The defendant was playing a game of chicken with jetliners." The court heard that Salamone had dived over homes, nearly collided with a police helicopter, and caused a security scare when he flew too near a local nuclear power station. Gradel also claimed that six aeroplanes had to be diverted by air traffic control to avoid a collision.

Salamone apologised and managed to smile as he was

handed his sentence. He had originally been charged with drink driving, but the charges were dismissed after a judge noticed that there was no state law dealing with drink flying. He was eventually jailed for 'reckless endangerment of life'.

DRUNK FRENCH COP DOES A SPOT OF MOONLIGHTING

A French policeman was forced

to admit to an interesting double life after being pulled over in his car, drunk and wearing nothing but a pair of fishnet tights. After a brief car chase through the seedy Bois de Boulogne area of Paris, the sozzled policeman explained that he was moonlighting as a male prostitute because he needed the extra cash. Although they charged him with drink driving, the authorities were somehow unable to charge

him with prostitution due
to 'insufficient evidence'.

LATVIAN ACHIEVES
WORLD RECORD IN
DRUNKENNESS

Eastern European countries
have produced some impressive
examples of drink-related
misadventure, but one
Latvian man went a step
further and achieved what

is believed to be the world record for being drunk.

The unidentified middle-aged man was found unconscious but in a stable condition by police in the capital city of Riga. A blood test showed his blood to alcohol level to be 7.22 parts per million. Ieva Zvidre, a police spokesman, explained that an average person would start vomiting at 1.2 parts, pass out at 3.0 parts and die at 4.0 parts. The head of the local hospital's emergency unit confirmed that there is no record, anywhere, of anybody surviving such a dose. "He won't remember a thing when he comes to," he added.

DRUNK DRIVER MAKES SLOW, UNSUCCESSFUL GETAWAY ON TRACTOR

When an Illinois sheriff found

a blue Chevrolet in a ditch with severe damage to its front end, he sped off to try and find the owner, who he believed would be walking along the road looking for help. When he returned to the car, empty-handed, he found the car's drunk owner, 40-year old Randall C. Jenkins, trying to pull his car out of the ditch with a tractor.

When challenged, Jenkins denied he had been driving the car and attempted to make his getaway on the tractor. A low-speed chase ensued, with the officer cruising behind the fleeing Jenkins at a leisurely pace. Eventually the chase ended at the home of one of Jenkins's neighbours, where he was seen to leap off the tractor and attempt to hide behind a shed.

The officer unsportingly marched straight behind the shed and arrested him, finding on him, amongst other things, a live kitten in his top pocket. "It's certainly a weird case," confirmed a police spokesman.

AUSTRALIAN COPS HOLD THEIR OWN IN PUB FIGHT

Police chiefs in Australia have been asking pub staff to report bad behaviour by off-duty officers after drunk cops were involved in a huge

96

bar brawl in the remote
town of Alice Springs.

Up to ten off-duty officers
were involved in the ruckus,
which took place after
a customer accidentally
stepped on one officer's
foot. It was also alleged
that a sergeant punched
the bar's chef in the back of
the head, and that a female
officer charged at the chef,
waving a bottle, as he tried

to get up from the ground.

An internal investigation took place but no criminal charges were filed after the bar's surveillance tape was deemed to be inconclusive.

DRUNKEN SAILORS DON'T SAIL FAR

Two United States Navy sailors were in hot water

98

after attempting a spot of
waterborne joyriding in the
Japanese port of Nagasaki.
The drunk duo, on their way
home from a boozy night out,
had the bright idea of stealing
a state-of-the-art fishing
trawler and taking it for a spin.

Alerted by staff of the seafood
company to which the trawler
belonged, harbour police sped
off in pursuit, only to find
that the boat had been run

aground 300 metres away. Inside, with nowhere to run, were the sailors. They later admitted to the theft, pleading extreme drunkenness.

'STEP OUTSIDE!' YELLS IN-FLIGHT DRUNK

A drunk Briton asking someone to 'step outside' for a fight is nothing out of the ordinary – unless it happens in an aeroplane. Thirty-year old Lee Rust of Plymouth was jailed for three months after necking a bottle of vodka before his easyJet flight from Alicante to Bristol and abusing fellow passengers. After Rust offered a passenger outside, an unfortunate crew member was forced to sit next to him to keep him calm for the rest of the flight, until he could be delivered into the hands of police upon landing.

DRUNK DRIVER SLEEPS THROUGH HIS OWN COURT CASE

When Gary Griffiths of Birmingham was accused of driving while five times over the drink-drive limit, everyone showed up to his trial but him. On the morning of his case, he was asleep in his solicitor's car after another heavy drinking session.

"He is fairly inebriated," explained Gary Griffith's solicitor. "Even if he came into court he might not follow proceedings. When he got into my vehicle he smelled of alcohol and then fell asleep. It takes a great deal of effort to wake him up."

The judge agreed to postpone the case until the next day, adding that Griffith was banned from driving any vehicle until then.

DRUNK IN CHARGE OF AN ELECTRIC INVALID'S BUGGY

A 74-year old Englishman has been banned from driving for 12 months after crashing his electric buggy into the back of a bus while drunk.

William Nolson, of Bradford,

was on his way home from the Shoulder of Mutton pub when the slow-motion accident occurred. He was carried, singing, into an ambulance and taken to Bradford Royal Infirmary where he was treated for a minor head injury and found to be well over the drink-drive limit.

"I'm packing in driving because I'm not fit to be on the road," the refreshingly honest Mr

Nolson admitted outside Bingley Magistrates Court. "I'm going to have an even more sheltered life now," he shrugged.

REVELLER THINKS OF NEW WAY TO BYPASS NIGHTCLUB BOUNCERS

An Australian man found himself regretting the volume of beer he'd drunk when he tried to sneak into a nightclub

through its air conditioning
system and got stuck.

The unnamed 20-year old
had been kicked out of the
Penrith Panthers nightclub
for drunken misbehaviour, but,
determined not to let that
spoil his night, climbed onto
the roof and through an air
vent. He then found himself
wedged in, head-first, and
remained there for six hours.

He was eventually rescued after calling a friend on his mobile phone, who alerted the emergency services. Authorities didn't prosecute the unnamed clubber, perhaps thinking that his ordeal had been punishment enough.

DRUNK MARTIAL ARTIST LOSES THE PLOT

Two police officers in Isla Vista,

California, responding to a late-night noise complaint at a block of flats, were puzzled to see two drunk men wrestling on the floor of the offending flat. They watched from outside for some time as the smaller of the men threw his friend around the place using various martial arts techniques.

After a few minutes, the officers slid open a window and demanded that they stop it and go to bed. Rather than comply, the martial artist good-naturedly asked the officers if they'd like to fight him themselves. The officers declined, but the man decided to fight them anyway and ran out onto the balcony in a karate stance, where both officers promptly pepper-sprayed him in the face.

Refusing to identify himself, the fighter was left in

110

an interrogation room at
the station to cool off.
Unimpressed, he stacked all
of the chairs in the room
into a heap and climbed up
it to try and hide inside the
ceiling. The duty officer found
him hanging out of the large
hole he'd created and whisked
him off to the County Jail
where he was charged with
resisting arrest, attempted
escape and vandalism.

DRUNK RADIO LISTENER MAKES UNUSUAL REQUEST

We've all been annoyed by local radio DJs before, but a drunk listener in the Russian city of Petropavlovsk-Kamchatsky took his irritation a step further than most. He armed himself with an air pistol and stormed the offices of the city's Radio 3 channel. Holding the pistol to the DJ's head,

112

the man demanded that he play his favourite song.

Understandably, the terrified DJ agreed and asked what the song was. The raider, however, refused to tell him. He then threatened to wreck the studio unless the DJ guessed correctly. Luckily for Radio 3 listeners, the police showed up and dragged the man off before he managed to vandalise the place. The name of his favourite song is still unknown.

LOCAL POLITICIAN LOSES SHIRT, TROUSERS AND DIGNITY

"I deeply regret that a personal issue has become so public," said Tom Coyne, former mayor of Brook Park, Ohio, after police released a video of him lying drunk in his garden minus his shirt and trousers. Responding to a call from a concerned resident, police had hauled Coyne out of his front garden on the night in question and found him to be three times over the drink driving limit. He had explained to them that he had thought he was at home in bed.

DRUNK HAS GREAT IDEA FOR HALLOWEEN COSTUME

It's one thing waking up in jail, the morning after Halloween, with a terrible hangover and no idea how you got there. It's quite another to learn that, the night before, you'd been wandering around a vastly crowded area with your wedding tackle hanging out of your trousers.

Police in Santa Barbara, California, were informed by a passer-by that a man was exposing himself in middle of a Halloween street party. Officers walked into the crowd to find the man standing there, reeking of alcohol, with his penis on full display, rambling unintelligibly and swaying from side to side 'with a dazed look on his face'.

On spotting the cops, he made

a fumbling attempt to put himself back in his pants, but was quickly grabbed and hauled off to jail, where, according to officers, he forgot the incident entirely within ten minutes.

AND FINALLY...

A drunk man was removed from a busy shopping centre in Germany after taking his clothes off and having sex with a blow-up doll in front of a horrified crowd of shoppers. Such was his determination to make love to his inflatable partner that it took some time for police to forcibly separate them, before charging the man with a whole host of offences. His partner, however, got away scot-free.

If you enjoyed reading this book, please visit our website to see what else we've published:

www.crombiejardine.com.

If you have any comments to make, or suggestions for other Little Book titles, please email: legless@crombiejardine.com.

All Crombie Jardine titles are available from High Street bookshops, Amazon, and Bookpost (P.O. Box 29, Douglas, Isle of Man, IM99 1BQ, U.K. Tel: 01624 677237, fax: 01624 670923, email: bookshop@enterprise.net. Postage and packing free within the U.K.)

The Little Book of Chavs

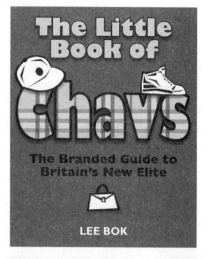

ISBN: 1-905102-01-1, £2.99

The Little Book of Chav Speak

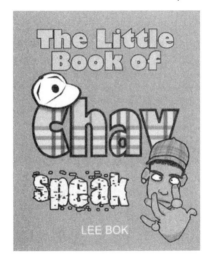

ISBN: 1-905102-20-8, £2.99

Shag Yourself Slim

ISBN: 1-905102-03-8, £2.99

The Little Book of Wanking

ISBN: 1-905102-00-3, £2.99

The Little Book of Bling!

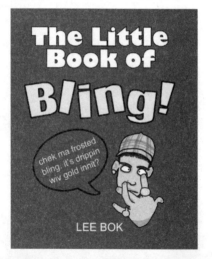

ISBN: 1-905102-21-6, £2.99

The Little Book of Goths

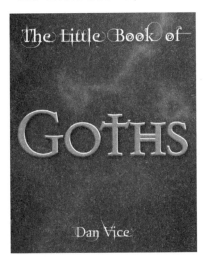

ISBN: 1-905102-24-0, £2.99

128

www.crombiejardine.com